COLUMBIA COLLEGE LIBRARY
600 S. MICHIGAN AVENUE
CHICAGO, IL 60605

3 2711 00178 7294

W9-CLN-898

JAN 1 9 2010

VIRGIL'S COW

FREDERICK

FARRYL

GOODWIN

VIRGIL'S COW

MIAMI UNIVERSITY PRESS. OXFORD. OHIO

MIAMI UNIVERSITY PRESS

356 BACHELOR HALL

MIAMI UNIVERSITY

OXFORD, OHIO 45056

Grateful acknowledgment is made to the following periodicals, in which poems in this collection have previously appeared: *Atlanta Review*: "Silent Movie with Vulture"; *Boston Review*: "Dr. Death" and "Virgil's Cow"; *Onsets (The Gig)*: "The Emperor"; *The Gig*: "Frost," "Margrave," "The Dualist," "Richard III," "The Occultist," *Harvard Review*: "Ophelia" and "Cannibal Rector"; *Incunabulum Records* (CD Booklet): "Violence," "The Porno Booth," "Hell's Angels in a Bar," "Woyzeck in Limbo," "Woyzeck in the Inferno"; *Into the Teeth of the Wind*: "Atheist"; *Margie: the Journal of American Poetry*: "McLean Hospital"; *North American Review*: "The Cardinal"; *Texas Review*: "The Butcher Shop"; *Worcester Review*: "The Crows."

Library of Congress Cataloging-in-Publication Data

Goodwin, Frederick Farryl.

Virgil's cow / Frederick Farryl Goodwin.

p. cm.

ISBN 978-1-4243-3113-0

I. Title.

PS3607.0592265V57 2009

811'.6—dc22

2008049418

FRONT COVER PHOTOGRAPH: TATSUYA,
BESTIA ANIMUS IN EFFECTUS, 1988
BACK COVER PHOTOGRAPH: TATSUYA,
EFFECTUS IN ABYSSUS, 1987
AUTHOR PHOTOMONTAGES: BRIAN MUSGROVE
AND SCRATCH PRODUCTIONS
DESIGN AND COMPOSITION BY QUEMADURA
PRINTED ON ACID-FREE, RECYCLED PAPER
IN THE UNITED STATES OF AMERICA

CONTENTS

1

2

5

Certain she heard the words—a human voice;

she saw a bird. And then she counted nine,

all talking crows . . .

OVID

1

OPHELIA

FOR LINDA

In Port-au-Prince your father made for you a pen of thorn
branches & a limestone crypt to shield you from cattle at night,
rowdy street life, the urban Voodou

culture of Elsinore. As though you were the last virgin cloud
forest midst the crumbling grand architecture of the Zona Colonial.
Midst mudslides & waterfalls,

. . .

you raced off to have your nose & clit pierced for rings, B-Girl!
from the Ocean's Edge, dense blue octaves of light stepped
like floodlamps into the steelworks

wreckage of your head & there by a crescent of moon! your
Father built for you an ark/ before the chambers of your
mind were flooded.

Lackey w/ a ring of Ophelia's posies : I fiddle w/ my chain of radiant keys : my duncecap:
my chimpanzees. You say no & I'll say yes.

You say yes & I'll say no. You order up a
recipe of blueskies & I rain on your parade(s). You bow down to the god

. . .

dess & I stuff a mushroom cap of harpies into your prayershawl. Tie your
tefillim to your head &heart & I'll senda

she wolf & vixen into Elsinore. Annoint all ofDenmark w/ the wolves of your indecision
& I'll send the gravediggers r & g [*H*] to snuff u out.

Is drowsy as a dog in the Petit Trianon, sniffing the rim of the sky for miraclez,
bovine taut to the Auroral R o a r. In his dreams he flies like a pot-bellied pig

uttering songs of undigestible beauty. Building complexcommunalnests
ofintricatelywovenvegetation like a weaverbird soured on sea tide .

∎ ∎ ∎

In the tall grasses he livesin MooMoo land, listening to the the muzak
of his own kazoo, under the broad-brimmed hat ofhis ownshapelyass

In the smkehouse, where waters change to wine, grass fires & snuff films

w/ halfclosed eyes in a seaofthyme the angels'scarlet mouths caroused beneath myudders

MANIFESTO FOR A GRAIN SHAFT

Pimple my tongue pellets w/ the Pharaoh's ten plaguesof pestilence!
I hang it mezzuzah-like on the ram's horn of my wife's hushed doorjamb

announcing the crack in the ancient clay jar of our brittle Domesticity.
Rummy extrodirnaire with an ace of spades jutting from my back.

. . .

I am on my back doing laps in the jar of my indolence.
A fin to aeroplane my blood boiling in the outback of faith.

Renounced in the D e a d S e a. The t in sha cks.

(I am) hermetically sealed against the twin typhoons of gravity and age.

HERE LIES THOUGHT

He is holding an *ark of opposites* within himself
broad as the Oshens-of-the-erth. while / Rommel & Remus w/ their hyena packs of
opposites: lie barely concealed beneath his amethyst muzzle, crowned by the "Pour le Mérite,"

[they r w/ o oars pruneinge aparttrees in a

cove of long house rows   picking apart meat , along a *Great Barrier Reef,*
in Modern Rome . Tart purple & orange. *Crushed to a hush.* Persistent. Vegetative.
stating our case before the Great Barrister , of the Lord's

miraculous Garden Gore, , skating on thin ice on his Ocean's floor, like a desert
of eternal electrical wonders circling the Egyptian's Sphinx
w/ its pyramidal configurations & rubric

cubes. Pharaoh, summoning ouir potentioner's phalanx
. . . .   of n=oble mathematicians . . . ,
muttering our calculus under starry skies.

THE CROWS

MOHEGAN BLUFFS, BLOCK ISLAND

Darting into our world
in their murmur of mourn cloth,
they come
peasant women
clicking their heels in unison,
mocking our slow flight.

I see them circling
a medicine wheel a friend
has built on a beach.
They land and carry off
the three guide stones placed in the middle,
later her uncle dies.

I see three crows
stand in the road outside a man's house.
His house is one of violence.
Soon he will pave the skies,
annihilate the mystery of silence.
Later things will happen.

THE EMPEROR

FOR NATE DORWARD

Should like to be responsible for the quiet elevation of the   quotidian
to icon. Given this gift as token from G–d for traveling along the toxic

rivers of our skin as warrior. He is working from a mineshaft formerly

lined w/ diamonds, once heavily radioactive, now hard wired directly to
the headdress of the sun.   To Whom, we go.

I glory in His name.
Melo drama.

■ ■ ■

THE RECORD

We are writing a record which will be read by few
but, yet, will be critical. At the intersection of life

and eternity stands death : with her hands crossed.
Still : she is dropping objects from her blouse like

apples from a purse. One by one.

■ ■ ■

We ripple in the breeze of her love. Blossom like indolent

children. Knowledge massing armies on the border.

RICHARD III

Du hast Diamanten und Perlen

HEINRICH HEINE

Mein Liebchen, Was Willst
Du Noch Mehr?

BORIS PASTERNAK

He is boiling the sky over London tonight, w/ his pink hairless arms full of soft bladk stars,
which he has crowned w/ onions, blistering the black meats.

One day! thinks, Will will also grow feet
on Fatty Arbuckle's cheeks b/4 he sleeps

■ ■ ■

Liebchen, stukk dukk, frozen in your boots & unable to houseflye w/ your
sack-of-rome-back dipped in arsenic, like a white hot watt, above the wounded fact

of England's frozen black waterz. Liebchen: to eat the white chocolate or the black?
The heart's courier : /: waits for you by the globe's standard received doors.

A [colony = colonial] jar of [of African Driver] bees funnels our excrement to the exhaust fans. Tough guys w/ .45's in each hand wreath their hearts w/ penis sheaths.

Outside, the Lone Rangers in their *testa roses* hum v's, [like] smother bruises left over from the gash o'oh a mother's absence, douse & delouse w/ rocket fyuel & kerosene.

        ■ ■ ■

I've cu t my voekel kords and sit myself on fire Aghain, a dirigible rising into a blue sky in a bathysphere Of saline Brine and the deep deep ocean of years

Sweep me up as a antler rackon topaFord Ram **1500** w/ a black **85** outboard in tow, tatooed left arm outside = [my] old black impala = somewhere down bonita rode.

I am shining cells in a cellar wrapped in cellophane. Fromthe bottom of the sea, I speak
eee-zee through a truncheon through a keyhole through a

throughway through a lopsided can with string attached, to another
57 varieties of ham. Glazed & glassy eyed

. . .

I shout "verboten!" w/ Erich von Stroheim
by my side & rise to the rafters from my depths Copper cukooo clock.

In the Dignitary's Mess, I change into tophat & tails w/ gluvs for dinner

m'luv. Rollw/ the tides outside. Seed the heath for poor tom/ther Titans' next monsoon

METAPHYSICAL LAP DOG

I am a bush pygmey & live in a forest without a horizon.
Traveling through such small spaces, I conclude from this that my fellow

man & me are the sport of Kings. And
that our Father who art in Heaven is one of us. One

∎ ∎ ∎

after the other we fall into a hole in the ground, O. Souki says.
It's enough to unsettle one's appetite for the sacred spice, I tell him. And yet,

according to our chief, a roll of the dice settles one down again.

He tells us to chant: "TO be close to you a s a lap dog. I'll carry your fleas."

<-|-|-|-|-|-|-|-|-|-|-|-|-|-|-

HEART

FOR LINDA

Dances with the Tushi Girls under a Blue Volcanic amoon &
Survives at world's end[1] & whileGathering w/ wild flocks of birds in

swoons smallrooms. Licks the envelope of the world before language,[2]
electrified fence,stored in a Red Houseby the Sexton's shed.

■ ■ ■

She is humming libations, swim w/ crustaceans, while whales[3]
as she faints by land'send Eating of the fathoms gushering up from[4]

She has Blended in w/ the woodwork. and the worms.joined forces[5]
melting the world into lariats. scentedw/ osprey .[6]

---

1. w/ the ratters to start again
2. bold as love, bolts from her
3. circle the -carp and -pistil in her head
4. springs beyondeye's jelly
5. w/ elected officials
6. or the hoopedtyphoons of lover's

FROST

Part of a moon was falling down the west as the hired man walked
along hedgerows in wild botanical bloom, fueled by ferocious gasoline,
carrying his down-turned downcast

iron smile to the bottom of the reverberant sea, like the oracular half
oval of an ancient wound, gardening his drainplug & dumpling of celestial
blood, bird-fluid in an oily depth

charge of Aviator's Air. Then, an orchid of nightfalls, each Mayan tooth
a fetish, pickling in a priestly brine, w/ his zinc placental overcoat rapt
upon his jungle's back, carpeting blue-green savannahs,

sexless as fire or a drum, w/ a fin of broken glass. The mast of mouth
indiscriminate as an inverted drunken ass, percolating to a boil,
he meant to clear the upper pasture too.

CANNIBAL RECTOR

I am sitting on a barge going downstream to Robert Mitchum's
house. Gamelan thimble cymbals adore my fleas.   All of

Hollywoodisthere. Little John and his den of wickedthieves
looting modern rome. Romeo ,adoring your lantern-like breasts.

You are the honey in the lion. I am the nut
w/ a crush.   A mouse runs

■ ■ ■

across the keys. The screen crackles for an instant
in the living room. i am d us ting for finger prints.

2

SILENT MOVIE WITH VULTURE

He wears the shrunken head of a large red man

and appears on the world's stage

fallen as an old Sioux Chief wearing the feathers of his war bonnet,

riding his white wimple

of air, roaring, wheeling like a pure metabolic alcoholic circling heaven on his unicycle

of sky

wrestling Ra.

Times have changed and with them tastes and so I have reduced,

(dare I say rescued?) the skillet's ingredients like a sous chef of irrational

exuberance to give you His Eminence Gris. Pure

vagrant undertaker

and hearse.

Content with the lion's garotte, the hyena's

appetite for breaking legs in dark alleys, the veldt's wide-angled

soup kitchen of destruction

and reproduction, he is all dark plumage, red neck tie

naked to the bone-through-the-nose ritualistic simplicity of the executioner's

Song of the Sun, Icarus taken on a blue trellis to a reading [room]

of the Egyptian Book of the Dead,

pages printed on the funerary papyrus

of skin,

gold-leafed, open to One.

■ ■ ■

And there, behind the black hood of feathers and stark red Phrygian
sailor's cap, unshaped as carrion, she stands : Shiva at the zoo with her death fan and six foot dihedral
cathedral of wing.

Angel-headed above earth's Gothic Swamp
she flies with Bishop's crosier, mice eyes diced like a master croupier, approaching
this thunderbird with a crop, who in such scrum
as scavenges earth's residuum, slouches towards eternity with buzzard's beak,
wild oars for feet ~ ~ ~ ~
and talons rowing towards the sun.

BLACK MAMBA

Green as death. The extinction caste. King of alchemy. Thee essence
of class. Jack's bean pole   at a school dance.   Master Wu's Walking

■ ■ ■

Stick. Green seraaaaaaaaaaaaaaaaaaaaaaaaaaaaaaaaaaaaaaaaaaaaaa(p)h.

TICK

Speak to the earth, and it shall
teach thee.

JOB 12:8

Swollen, they resemble
Bosch's fruit, or FALLEN —

tiny anglers w/ harpoons,
from the apple orchard's

second tree, beyond duality,
with its roots : outside

the Hassid's House of
good and evil's Neural

Angels, who bear . . .
their chalice of blood

in a simple pale green
nut to the floor of the

flower room with the legs
of tumescent adolescents,

tucked back like Friars
from the world at large.

Their heads as black
as faint pin pricks . . .

the antithesis of their
former selves. Now,

Skeletal *as* October trees—
downwind the PIG FARM.

VIOLENCE

Man must kill man
for his mouth was originally a mollusk,
which spoke only Latin,
and yearned, in its thirst, to drink
in its entirety, the living ocean.

■

My dream is to go somewhere,
somewhere exotic and stimulating,
and be murdered. The thugs,
whom I adore.

■

I have married the walking uterus
with the snake. In the outhouse
of my male hysteria, I am on a stage
fulfilling my therapist's fantasy
that I impersonate Saddam Hussein.
I am in thrall to the whoredom,
of impersonality.

■

In America, darkness and the blubber
of black fields, surrounded by the sour odor
of greens. Vincent's crows loose
in a burlap bag, clutched to the wound.
The original wound which bled Mary
and all over the living, Christ. Beuys
on a tram platform. Under swirling, starry
fluorescent nights, I am gazing into nothing,
from a carousel, a ladder between my teeth.

■

An 800 foot long snake, writhing from the ether
of my impending absence, dances on a stage,
inside the apple of my tree, sawn in two,
inside my head.

■

Do not think there is not hunger in the world
that the sheep and lamb are slaughtered needlessly
that man is not sundered from his soul
to appease the appetite of those who hold
up the catacombs of the living sun, and the world
with its termites, sticks covered with sticky cloth,
Lord Honey with his whims.

■

One pisses on a father's grave with equal
amounts of prudence and modesty. A touch
of zeal is, on occasion, not out of place.

■

In late autumn, I set myself on fire again.

■

I gave you my love where you had none. But
now you must sit with your sister Time. For
my wrath is greater than even hers, and my love
more severe even than that.

■

One could die in Berlin, in Paris, in Jerusalem
even, the smell of rank death on one's fingertips,
again, settling into one's bones, rocking it
as one might a baby, giving birth to one's opposite,
newborn.

■

One gives up one's family with hesitation, and only
after great deliberation, the burden becoming too much,
the oily fishheads surrounding the small boat one
has been forcibly set in, calling like sirens, broken
in their grief.

I suspect my original colour was red
and that I am a yellow wave at my crepuscular cellular core.
Not rotten as some would have me think.
Ich haber hunger.

I will take a cruise ship to nowhere with a woman
whose name cannot be pronounced within the sand
trap of any language already invented without one's
body bursting into a pillar of frozen salt at high noon.

I had breakfast this morning with Gary Cooper.
He proposed to me instead of Grace Kelly.

The title song, *Oh Susanna,* is commingling with the Anton
Karas score from *The Third Man.* I can't tell if I'm in the OK
Corral or postwar Vienna. I think my name is Holly Martins
though I look like the little Austrian who plays his seedy
violin in the cabaret beside tables of *Herrs* and *Frauleins.*

WOYZECK IN LIMBO

[IN FLOATING AQUATIC TUTU]

Circles, his mother suggests.
    <They're good.>

           Herr Soy says you begin where you end,
                <he protests.>

                        He knows   *He made*
                        <me . . . in his Knefle Factory.>

BACON

Goya
is at his desk:
besieged
by 20th century
demons.

■ ■ ■

A skillet
of steak n'
onions,
. . . a slice
of kidney
or eel pie,
stink up

the cell block.
Rhubarb, smears away
the tears.

"I can't tell
if everything is too close,
or too far away,"
he shouts in the dark.

"It's perpetual night!"
he cries.

Skin
almost like a new religion.
(I think I'll convert)
Like rennet . . . melting from pork rinds,
beautiful, as a parasol,
he/she fought/thought
Or the sun,

setting over slaughter.

THE PORNO BOOTH

In the dry grasses,
by the rushes of every city,
you can find it:

the edge of a cliff.

Where the lonely gather
as if in dreams,
to practice the rites,
of their small phosphorescent
sleep.

Here, far from the shelter
of a city's makeshift lean-to's.
Far from its MEN'S BARS and strip joints,
tattoo parlors SAILOR'S BARS,
greasy coffee nooks and steamy
hot dog stands   *Far from the*
loneliness of its dance
halls and night clubs,
receding at this moment
like a melody,
above a far-off town.
The descent of human
hands, tonged to trousered laps,
and then, beyond,
into the troughs of worlds
below this one:

There, Safe from the Flowers of Spring
The blue Swords of Iris
The mud of Mad Rivers
Safe from the Fires of Silence
Safe from birth
The birthing of spring
The tender Altar Rites of iris
Safe from the terrible Long Horn of Light
Nakedness and song—
Burning in the Mystery of the Orchard

The concrete bride
of the city's huge groin
Rears by the bush of her soft ruin
coughing rubble, steel, and tar.
The dark blaze of her bright bison blood
pulsing heavily, in the arteries,
above each sweaty storefront, which steams
like warm neon.
She burns in her cold trough.

There, huddling in hives-of-cold,
furring the walls with sweat:
stalls of men breeding
furiously: with themselves.
Men too lonely, for women,
singing the body electric,
in dread: outside of bed.
Watching.

The sound of one hand clapping.

THE BUTCHER SHOP

Frocked as a friar in white cloth,
when he opens each morning,

cheeks red, lips calm,

he stands in the midst of dull vertical
propellers, as if in a hangar,

awaiting his descent.

In his little shop of horrors,

there is music:

harps wired of sinew and nerve,
backs, strung evenly with bone,

like xylophones.

Like a whaler, he knows the tropics in his box of red tide
and slaps the smooth blue pimpleless hocks

of the young underwater,

like an amphibious Mother, in the wrong place,
at the wrong time . . .

But that's not all:

The butcher also knows the calm secrets,
of madmen.

And has listened to the choir,

hanging, from the sly pew
of his rafters: toe-ganged

and nailed, a gothic red nightmare,
on a stainless steel stave.

A conductor, he notches bone
till it sings antiphonally,

as any chorus cantorum,
poises his eager torso over pink hairless rumps and,

in full view of patrons, skillfully snaps entrails free

from political places, in a Confucian fanfare,
of fantastic fist fucks.

He has fingered the pig girl's brown eyes
clean, of their light, so many times,

he never bothered to count,
catastrophes. And shaves children back

to butter, under the swing of his blade.

Balloon Man,
Emperor of Ice Cream,
Isambard Kingdom Brunel: Move Over.

In the butcher's aquarium
of red blood, the white-frocked

Friar of Carnage hangs his tablecloth

vertically, officiates post-mortemly
in the community.

Like us: is privileged to know the tale
of the lamb, with the eye of a tiger,

while dispensing stealthily

from a shop on the block,
on an unseen altar,

tiny offerings

bleeding from a galaxy's
remote corner

noiselessly.

HELL'S ANGELS IN A BAR

AMSTERDAM 1984

They could be Vincent's *Potato
Eaters*, gods of negation, kilted
in chrome, and strutting upon
a highland of need,
bootleggers of boyhood
chromium whores, or
virgins in a drum roll sleep.

I'M AN IRAQI TOO

I'm sweating like a Roman Diva:
ingesting Saddam's Greek flies.
His spirit clings to me like a cheap
suit in thin air. My flesh is a side
of radiant ham, infused with rare spices,
radioactive with the Chemist's cornucopia,
ancient suitcases with their asphalt
alphabets of paper wasps which fly.
The Periodic Table of Elements dispenses
the ghosts of the dead on its Ouija Board.
The living clean the windshield,
with Sophocles' swords.

HARD CORE

But as if a magic lantern threw the nerves in patterns on a screen.

ELIOT

In the drab display of the porno arcade
ten thousand leagues beyond,
Eros and Psyche loiter like tourists:
lost in a totemic theme park.

Doctors, lawyers, Indian Chiefs
men without skin: Elephant-men,
Aladdins and alchemists rubbing their lamps,
seeking the taproot, mining for gold,

tossing tokens into a wishing well
hell. These are men mesmerized
by their homunculi, a pavilion of millions
who are noisily oiling their vermillion-red horns

like Vikings, with a quiver, quaffing
gravity in a prehistoric meat cove.
Patrons of porn
these are the custodians of civilization's norms

who follow like blind sheep, deaf shepherds
of vast heat, ushers of lush landscape
millers of dead seed.
There, from a Magic Lantern's

incandescent moor, midst steep chasms
the world's bed-sitters watch,
like whores along a watchtower
who ascend in arterial splendour

panting in need, from a dark square
of Bedlam, riding bareback
behind a vast door. Gentle lord,
take these *Blaue Reiters*, horse necks gorged

with veins of deep greed
and bathe them in your irradiated splendour.
These lost who learned not to grieve,
their primordial loss of Promethean need.

Testosterone junkies who molt like immortals.
These *Titans* dying of thirst at a celestial spring.

THE MAD ARE EXOTIC

Flagellants in an arctic dark,
they play their withering
spoons beneath the tender
belly of a dustbin
moon, distilling silence,
spiritual alms, the Furies'
acetylene perfume.

MOSQUITOS

Like Roald Dahl's character Henry Sugar,
whom they can see through the blindfold-of-skin, the wagers-of-fear,
the control-of-sin like Indian Fakirs

∎

in a casino, chips piled high for the blood count,
the fast fillies filling up on pro tein at the pump. Males make doin
their private Motel Rooms

∎

plastered on horse hair & tall gr asses. Waving their tails over the
moisture of sap dropped from leaves, their young gorging on
pickpocket's loot, they reach w/ needle

∎

nose pliers for the high test of their e-lectric Eucharist.
Cowgirls w/ long lariats flail the spinning earth:
then the rushing   of the Rodeo Bulls.

HEAVY METAL

The roots going below ground to Beowulf. Green harvested from beets. The willow out back dies a slow death. Branch by branch.

FLYING SAUCER

Vitek Spacek pounding on the door with Polish day glow hair. Which concealed a thing still emerging from ice.

THE SIRENS

You know it's not you they're coming for this time. I am moved to comment on the killing of a man.

ADULTERER'S SKYSCAPER

greenhouse gases

big black heart

monkey tree

mona lisa light

man with a big shadow

red handed man

masked man

man with a porcupine quill

IM: THE ROBOT GEISHA

Waits for the men from the city, appearing at her door like
gorillas from lowlands,
to feast on the soft succulent inner shoots of her bamboo, so
that she may

fan away their heat, in the recess of the rainy season, as she
reclines
on her nebulae of sensuous order. Porcelain painted *high-serene*
as her innermost triptych

. . .

paneled screen featuring her neon metaphysical fatigue : green
garden arbour of Basho's languor, stepping with bound feet wound
with butterfly string

of the Cadillac Void, wearing the yakuza's red lady slippers,
as she waits for the men to come in, like Adam w/ his hurt
sounds. & His devastating feral fury.

THE SALESMAN

(OF ADVERTISING SPACE)

On a good day, he is the great god OZ,
the wizard so wizened he is no longer hybrid
or half human but the thing itself, MERLIN'S
pure wand, the dust bowl's down-to-earth feedlot
of wisdom, pitch perfected to a piccolo's high
diminuendo, hermitage of rhetoric's lapidary facets,
he is shimmering with a trout stream's easy iridescence
trunk-solid as a mountain man, urbane purveyor
of seraphic implication, a dowser of water
drowning sorrow, dispeller of foot-thick
fog, the white picket fence by the water's
edge, an Aztec effigy, clubfoot of grace,
a caricature of certainty, the orphanage's
maze and cavern, its eternity of dark grace.

In an ancient voice, he is the sole auditor
of our ambivalence, Jehovah's witness,
in a Consultant's smug room, its flood of horizons
its hat rack of moons, its hat trick of impressive credentials
the jungle's candelabra
of sunrise, its credenza of baboons
the long, erectile crest of a cockatoo
Parrot set to classical Noh drama,
the orient's painted orb,
a languid offering of porcelain serenity,
pure Japanese.

He is the KING OF COMEDY,
performing on a yellow brick road
a burlesque striptease on skid row,
drinking *Veuve Clicquot,*
Château d'Yquem with his *crème brûlée* or
Night Train, Thunderbird
Ripple glazing his eye, with his Sara Lee micro-waved apple pie
on a sub par week, but still tuned to perfect pitch
in a HYATT, FOUR SEASONS EXECUTIVE SUITE
USED CAR LOT, CRUMBLING MAI TAI LOUNGE,
where he remains the star attraction of picture power
the spearhead of rhetoric properly contained, patiently but not portentously enameled
with the majesty of gravity, the pendulous R RATED HYPNOTIST
of credibility in a small room, yodeling
in gravity's spittoon, Tarzan
calling for Jane under a city bar's
cheap BUDWEISER MOON.

Epistle

to a Minyon

Composed

of

Monteverdi	*Elgar*	*Thomas Tallis*
Krishnamurti	*Martin Buber*	*Baal Shem Tov*
Jack in the Pulpit	*Nick Cave*	*James Brown*

———

Lovely with their sportcoats, and garter belts
spiking and lilting to the heavenly spokesof
the milky way and those chrome spokes which
buttomed down to engines steam coming out

of fluted exhausts and the one hundred and
thirty two vibrqation of a bass guitar humming
its harmonics in the tall grasses of the ancient
hall spoke of this cast of hundreds which paraded in and

out in and out in and out of the front door od this litle shop
of horrors each and every week returning too weak to even
smile at this group which manned the hatches and acted as if
eye contact would turn the world to stone.

———————————

Charlotte Mew   *David Dabydeen*

Marilyn Nelson

James Brown

————

As a hat and an adult duiaper while he drivshis ark to the king
dome of his peers he swears his years are melting away in america's
melting pot whose strs and stripes are smeared with the other warpaints
ion his cherokee cheekbones he is a black hassid in hiding from his village
elders who cheriub his butts with annointing oiuls and pigmeants from the chief
mospuito by the creek with no name burning boiling oil.

———————————————

שרצסלס דנא שמרס ללא ה הו נ רעהתע יוסדאהש ש הת ס שנס תאתנעשׁערפער ענ ש ד תצב ערע

תש מ שצס רעתשימ עהת נ שדנאה ס תעש נעעשנצ נא יב דעח מ גנ עב ערעו

שעש ל דעש ל ילעתאארעפשעד ר עהת ס

ס ר עהת ילעתאארעפשעד דעש ל שעש ל

ערעו גנ עב דעח מ יב נא נעעשנצ תעש ס שדנאה נ עהת שצס רעתשימ תש מ

ערע תצב ענ ש ד שנס תאתנעשׁערפער ס ש הת יוסדאהש רעהתע נ ה הו ללא שמר דנא שרצסלס

Were but divine representations of this shadowy ether in which all forms and colours

were being mixed by an unseen set of hands in the mysterious mist

of their desperately lived lives

lives lived desperately their of

mist mysterious the in hands of set unseen an by mixed being were

colours and firms all which in ether shadowy this of representations divine but Were

פעעש יעהת שא תצסהנגצסרהת דנא שללא ער לס צב שת ו גנ ננ נעב עהת מסר שעננאה נס ת ד עה
ית עהת סתנ נ רעפעעד דנא רעפעעד

רעפעעד דנא רעפעעד נ סתנ עהת ית
עה נס ת ד שעננאה מסר עהת גנ ננ נעב ו שת לס צב שללא ער דנא תצסהנגצסרהת שא יעהת פעעש

The diction changes from the beginning w/ its bucolic recalls and throughout as they seep

deeper and deeper in intoi the city

city the intoi in deeper and deeper

seep they as throughout and recalls bucolic its w/ beginning the from changes diction The

נג לפצס רצעתצא ס דנ כ א ש רעה דנא מ ה ס ששענשצס שנס עהת נעעותעב נס תאנרעתלא עהת
דעתאלצננא רת ס דנ כ א
נס תאלצפס

the alternation between the consciousness of him and her is a kind of auteur coupling

a kind of triangulated

copulation

WOYZECK IN THE INFERNO

[IN BURNING SAFFRON ROBE]

The Buddha is cleaning spider webs from the window

       In the garage, are two bicycles, a sun and a moon.

                                   The garden hose funnels water to where it's needed

                                                . . . his right hand bleaches the sky.

CHELSEA

"Closing time," sings the Mariachi band. Three Spanish
royals at the bar w/ earmuffs & beards. Crying in their negra
modelos @ La Tijuana on Broadway.

It's cold at midnight by Fitzgerald Shipyard @ the end of
Winnisimmet. Las putas stroll by the old water hole and propane
tanks. The D.P.W. mounds its

arsenic-laced pillar of white salt. The freighters steam under
the Tobin & Winnisimmet like thugs surrounded by a
mob of red tugs. The produce section

rots in a refrigerator w/ the strippers @ St. Arthur's Court.
"The wolf of winter will soon be at our throats," one
besotted otter throws out

while Richard Brautigan puts down his cerveza
and walks out the door /,\ trolling
in the gutter for rainbow trout <++++

3

MORMON STOCKPILE

WATER

Bottled water (gallons)—
Stationary supply—well water? (have tested)

FOOD

Main (Protein, Carbohydrate, Fat)

Beans (cans, black)—32
Beans (cans, pinto)—
Salmon (cans)—34
Ravioli (cans)—

Side (Vegetable)

Corn (cans)
French green beans

Side (Soup)

Tomato
Chicken noodle

Toilet paper (rolls)

Rubbing alcohol

Toothpaste

Paper towel

MCLEAN HOSPITAL

BELMONT 1970

It was the gold standard
of High Society.
Promising silver service
to platinum-plated,
Martha Stewart
mental cases (like me),

with their Tiffany
silver suitcases full of silver
spoons, the country club set
with ants on their faces
sprawled,
on cricket lawns.

The little Marquis
with his 3-piece suit,
wearing wing tips. Growing
buffalo wings.
The Monsignor therapist
with his

epic odes for lost souls,
haikus of (weekend)
aristocrats swimming their laps
in their private lakes.
The hospital's extravagant,
isolation tanks.

HEAD HOUSE

1

Has historically prided itself on never assigning rooms to its occupants.

2

It's the kind of risk-taking concept that not every house can pull off.

3 A

Shakespeare / among others / sought to imbue the house w/ a sense of mystery.

3 B

And to this day still points to the front door / a slab of glass
hung on offset pivots / which allows a visitor to see through the house
and out into the landscape beyond / as the kind of detail
that anchors the house in the early 21st /
rather than the early 17th century.

An inventory was once taken which revealed that it contained
a straw bed to lie down on & a man overboard.

Life rafts were designed
w/ the buiding and / at the christening of the first ships / it was suggested
by the Admiral of the Royal Cloud Fleet / that things "were generally . . .
intended to go w/ the ice flows".

Others in the vast crowd offered that the organs
of state might contribute to the overall effect & editing processes /
which take place w/ in the passel
of grand guest rooms.

The farmers in their muddy boots / and potato-stained overalls /
let it be known that large red tractors / w/ slightly noirish riders /
would thresh the seas of waving grain / when necessary /
below low lying horizontal clouds, whose domed summits
might alternately inflate to promise fruit or threaten rain /
in the convenience of the distance.

8

Finally / track lights w/ faulty wiring were installed to twinkle below
a starry ceiling to allow for the panhandling of ivory / abalone and whalebone.

9

From less enlightened times / the devil in a horse-drawn wagon /
I'm told / persuaded the owner to finally upgrade / which is why
despite being surrounded on all sides by heavenly choirs /
you can / some days / still catch a glimpse of hell.

DREAM HOUSE

The locals say, remains buzzing with bees, whispering of
intimate ancient harmonies. Twisting shallow stairs set sail each
night which spiral further upward, where

■

Jesus passed the Crucifixion Fountain, Dante the Holy
Paradise Fountain, and Jacob Boehme the Fountain of Life. It's sometimes
rumored that Novalis passed the Blue

■

Flower Fountain, Crane the Bridge Fountain, and that Henry built the
Sad Lullaby Fountain of his dreams here. Centuries later, the
boundary to its precincts was extended

■

as it continued to draw the first families, who were Petroleum
Pall Bearers. All w/o sacrificing, I can attest, any
of its original rustic charm.

MASADA HOUSE

"Where have all the wise guys gone?" cries Herod, from
the Bath House. Hoards of shekels at his feet, women in white togas w/ braided hair

dropping grapes into the mouths of men, pooling in the intricate mosaics laid in the floor
of the Playboy Mansion's infamous grotto. The remains of a cloth bag adhering to the coins,

■ ■ ■

two milleniums later & stuccoed to his back in 4 B.C. when he dies. 70 years later fame,
like a livery, delivers the tar vat to the mountaintop w/ Rome's Heart wound

up to tick like a nervous song in the birdhouse of summer.
Masada's teeth overlooking America's own dark mansions and Dead Sea.

While water-crowned the zealots drove their burning rains
across the smoking plumes & twin towers of an arid plane.

GRAVE HOUSE

At 4,000 feet there's a dispensary for lychee nuts
& the Korean farmers, whose parents moved here in the 1950's,
harvest watermelons on its northern steppe,

.

where the Great Meadow w/ its leeching bed sprawls above
and below the house w/ white daisies & tiny wild roses
of the old souls. A white-headed eagle

.

circles overhead ignoring the carrier pigeons, bearing news
of other worlds. In a field of poppies, a young Tatar girl
lays the groundwork for a home of limestone,

.

while in the beginning, only men were allowed
inside to care for the dead, beating
their heads w/ stones.

HERR WORM BARON

Herr Worm Baron speaks w/ a sapphire whisper counting
the seven gazelles of the senses in his sleep, before he eats. In
his house, the parlor furniture

is shrouded in a canopy of belladonna beneath the forest floor.
He reckons the world is his to dust. "Ooof w/ their heads, oof w/ the rust!"
he is known to implore

. . .

w/ his now famous roar. Through the flues of his chimneys, our
smoke mixes w/ his hibiscus snores. Garlands of lice scamper
like mice as his nostrils exude

their infamous *spice*. Down into the depths of time's slums,
the high Magistrates come. Bearing letters of transit,
letters of silence for some.

EVE'S HEART

FOR LINDA

Dances naked w/ the Tushi Boyz & Girlz
under a blu volcano moon,
to survive w/ the rats at Headlands End

to start again, fanning (fuming) up
in her wild bearded arms flocks of birds in small
rooms. "A tuba for the John Philip

Sousa(s), measuring two by two" she croons
a Perry Como Hour gothic
chanteuse humming libations,

swimming w/ crustaceans, as whales circle
the electrified fence sound=surrounding the Sexton
in the Red House, stored on the headdress

& hard drive of her feathered Crow Head.
She had almost managed to blend in
w/ the woodwork & the worms

as she joined forces w/ elected officials,
afloat in the brine of one,
or another, of His/ or /Her atmospheric airs,

as if her (the) gesture might finally Melt
the world into lariats, which she had Scented
w/ osprey, as she fainted w/ A. by

Lands End, holding the hooped-typhoons-
of-lovers, burning like midnight oil,
inside the lamp-of-the-world

of her iPod.

■ ■ ■

I'M A SPANIARD TOO

1

¿Que pasa? ¿Estás bien? / someone asks at midnight.

2

Families with small children dressed in white are walking on the promenade which skirts the sea.

3

Yo soy un pece / I respond / *I am a fish.*

4

The sea affects everything about me / collects information on me / pumps saltwater through my unfathomable gills.

5

All summer / I listened to flamenco in Madrid's cafes / Now / I sleep under the stars
with my new German girlfriend Kossa by the little harbour where we fish.

6

We come here each night after dancing in the local discotheque till 4 a.m.

7

My parents are nudists / she confides / and strips naked to the bone
on the beach at every opportunity.

8

Weed is growing wild / and is trimmed by the gardeners / with the hedgerows /
at La Universidad de Santander / where we are both taking classes.

9

When we wake by the harbor in Del Monte / we can only think about getting
high in Los Picos de Europa / The bull crumpling like black crepe under the matador's cape.

The cave containing Andalusian sunsets set on fire at dawn.

The Queen's English setting sail with Columbus and a spear.

Taino / Nahuatl / and Maya in the hold / on the voyage home.

4

LIGHT AND DARK IN AN ESCHATOLOGY

BASED ON THE ALPHABET

Bidden or unbidden, G–d is present.
SIGN ABOVE JUNG'S DOOR

a —— See saw
. . . G . . . ,

b — on its way
. . . to Z . . . ,

c —— pausing,
only long

d — enough,
to remind

e —— I, that
O is wide

f — enough,
in Heaven,

g —— for Yes,
and No.

THE CARDINAL

From the sun room
I am the first to hear

his staccato call
of notes,

vivid pluck of pizzicato
or soliloquy

and spot the Roman
triple crown, red-capped tiara,

by the sunflower feeder
in the ground

the Colossus
in a coliseum of *blue blue*

indigo sky, small twin propeller
airliner, by the fallen throne

of our backyard. His mistress,
is a small brown goddess

in fall, whose mitered
head blows past the fleeting

air like some
small miracle

of dust dressed in her husband's
robes of red

and borne of the season's mystery
in flight

newly sprung from the garden's
larval bed.

When I was young, I was a fish & swam through incandescent oceans, through women
to the kingdom of a god, and then face to face, an astronaut in outer space. We shook

hands, expressed our love for one another, out of life in the everlasting. He asked what
kind of car would a creature like me be after. If not one with fins—& *ah black exhaust?*

■ ■ ■

ANCHORS

I was drinking the sky through a straw. Blue sky
and the din of Montana. Never been there, never
want to. Oceans away from my kind of sailing . . .
I'm peeling off my skin, from the inside, each day
that I'm here, pouring earrings all over my body,
map of the world each time I cross the horizon,
the hundred or so times I've been right hear:
the hundred or so times I've been right theirs.

DOUBLE ZERO LAND

There is a grand river running   through the disposition
of my faith. For I have seen rich men die at their desks,

of heart attacks, and carry on like ghosts through generations.
It is as it should be. Quiet.   In the stalls. The immortals tread

    ■ ■ ■

elsewhere. It is their right. I count loose change in words
Drink the beverage of the sky.   Carry on with a farmer's

work. Mucking out the I.

THE *ATHEIST*

I imagine you at twilight
fingering the wind, as if the
broad-beamed breath of the
world were your own,
your hands ringed with water
drawn from a nearby well,
and your face staring past me,
as if carved of indolent stone.

.is in the gravel pit of the five senses with the mongoose and the cobra .climbing
the ladder of Almighty Fire in ethereal drawing rooms

He is flying to Mecca and Medina in the morning, having risen with Mohammed on the Dome
of the Rock to Highest Heaven.

        ■ ■ ■

plucking white feathers from the black crow in his office on the fourteenth floor
of Southwark Tavernpulling gold teeth from the other pilgrims like old holes soldered to the

wooden floors and filo of souls. into the blue never never land of ether and sky.
Is. At the Gates of Paradise, cantering into canterbury singing

THE BIGAMIST

How (is it that) water turns to fire and, then,

the gas chamber(ed heart) of the sun and,

then, finally, (to) love? I learned to eat in

rooms with my heart cut in two and share(d)

myself in equal halves with people and with

G–d, like a bigamist with a hole in his soul,

the size of earth.

UNTITLED

Here, where we read the Braille
of the stars, under the Eucharist
of sky. Drunk, eternity surrounds
my head, like a lantern of light.

The moon's deep waters pour the
cistern of the sky. And the page
turns softly in the breeze, quiet
as the centuries.

1

Within the cut field, a plow
being pulled at night. The
tiller of a thousand notes,
is silence.

HEMLOCK

The wind lashes our faces in early
November, a head of the snow.

The garland of green heads who brought us spring burned in summer.
Bummer. Who knows where they might have taken us after December?

        ■ ■ ■

5

BARDO HOUSE

ASSEMBLAGE/FOUND TEXT ON PAPER

In the beginning / only women were allowed inside to care for the dead.

■

Carefully wrapping the corpses / painting their faces white /
as the spirits gathered outside / waiting to come in.

■

From the antique / cream-colored globe lamps
to shiny chrome spigots / its forlorn waterfront is prewar
and proletarian / to its totemic fetish of a core.

■

One of the keys to the rise in its reputation as a countinghouse /
and old-fashioned greengrocer / is its diamond industry.

■

Located at opposing ends of its central atrium / on a soaring staircase
woven of vellum & gilt-edged leaf / it retains & honours its proud tradition / as distribution
point for old world commodities

■

And the soluble soul / whose pulp Tuvan whalers / ferry to Trade route sailors
from wild waves /:/ to starboard sleep.

■ ■ ■

Mere migrant worshipping at the pygmy's Herculean thirst.
Drawn on this canvas, tied out of bounds by the flotsam's sheared end,

by the discus flight of an unsandaled heart, I seek the way to the mile after Mecca.
Collect the nether world in my tin cup of daylight, act as beacon to the obdurate waves.

. . .

Of her heavenly spoke, is a papoose of glimmering meteor showers,
loosed from the necklace of divine Grace. Long live the partridge in the pear tree,

of her gentle heart. Surely, in such glacial melt is where pearls
were cast, before the swine of apes.

This is my monsoon, begat of Abraham, Isaac and Jacob,
the hole in my heart the size of a burning bush, quivering nightshade,

deadly to the tongue in the outback of my lie. Japanese is the leaf eyeing the toadstool of my
anus, pelt the soil at the loose end of my fingertips, stamen to the branches greying under the

■ ■ ■

armpits of my neanderthal soul. Chariot is the spring given the lyre playing under the
pomegranate by the loadstar of nectar pulsing in the pumice, dust of my cavernous murmur,

deadly as the heart's symphony loose as a goose in a sky of Canadian tundra, maritime by the
buoy of my mouthings lost on the unquenchable, changeling tides of the soul's bitter fruit.

They come to visit in dark suits speaking Portuguese.
Bearing tropical fruits, the sea's briny bread loaf.

Sugar magnetized to the maggots of the stars glistening overhead
in the headdress, crown of thorns, black blood oozing the nightshirt

■ ■ ■

over the magnetic torso of day to which we pin our singed hopes.
Sing aloud for the crops of our farming to turn the fields of our lives

into edible manna in the throes of our famine. Repeat from the farmer's last page of testament.

I am liquid in a water play, seaside with nothing to say, abject   in the isolation of my serenity.

DR. DEATH

You unearth me. And sendme packingback to the orbiting
tern of the self. You glo=itterr by the ocean's edge, out beyonfd Edgar's cape.

Go! make your appointed
roiunds. Painted dignitary

. . .

to the apothecary.
Chemist with a thousand stars in each eye.

Your pigskin freckles tickle me. Your heart built of a million spears

on fire. Noiseless as a printer without power.

HORACE'S HIPPOPOTAMUS

Iz half-out-of-dream-water-down-on-Maecenas' farm,
w/ the weight of the late ancient world anchored to the borders
of each imperial shoulder and the shorelines

.

of the Caliphate's Interior Sea. He blows a reedy mixture
of red cake and celestial muck from his Byzantine Ass, munching
on the latin *Quintus Horatius Flaccus*

.

from the white house and ocean-lined hut of his sleep. Then,
hauling himself onto dry ground, remembering his debt
to his Father, he asks one of eight laborer

.

slaves whether sugar peas wrestle along a trestle with the
honey bees, if the pubic halo of a girl's sugar nova
shines in the midday sun

.

outside Rome in Green Country, whether other Hippos
might care to guzzle his jolting caffeine While Contemplating
the infinite expanse and the Axis of Evil

.

which lies beyond borders like an archer shooting arrows
fashioned from the tips of a harlot's miraculous lips. Paddling
upstream, panhandling for the gold-

∎

leaf strophes of immortalized odes, e iz a King on horseback
mouthing the saviary aviary of his plankton-rich home,
While Of the Empire he writes: wired

∎

wildly to it is a wild god poised to dive *into-the-drain-
pool-of-his-dreams:* whose couplets once rhymed
with a woman's moist kiss,

∎

who dowsed for water ploughing Rome's animal soul under:
I, who could not fathom that Christ's rain would fall
in the ancient world to the rumblings of Augustan Thunder.

Ab la dolchor del temps novel
Foilloli bosc, e li aucel
Chanton, chascus en lor lati,
Segon lo vers del novel chan;
Adonc esta ben c'mon s'aisi
D'acho dont hom a plus talan.

With the sweetness of the new season
The trees put forth their leaves, and the birds
Sing, each in their own language
Following the measure of the new song:
Therefore it is well that a person take possession
Of that which he most desires.

GUILLAUME DE POITIERS

I would like to acknowledge the following people:

Sincere gratitude to **NATE DORWARD**, *my editor,*
for his exceptional expertise, guidance, and patience

JEFF CLARK, *my designer, visionary seer of the printed page*

LINDA *without whose love, friendship, & infinite*
kindness this book could not have been written

DAVID, *a friend*

DAVID SCHENCK, *reader, whose early unsolicited support was a gift*

Dedicated to the memory of my good friend **THOMAS C. MCGOWAN**

& the memory of my mentor **DEREK DOWSON**,
St. Edmunds College, Cambridge Founder

DAN WARBURTON, KEN WADNESS, KATHLEEN SPIVACK,

DANA LEONARD, MARILYN GOODWIN, BRAM GOODWIN,

FRED/BETH ERLICH, RAY DINITTO, TOM/JOHN DIMITROFF,

PROFESSOR SAMUEL J./ARLENE BERNSTEIN & MY FAMILY.

FREDERICK FARRYL GOODWIN

WAS BORN IN 1953 IN FRAMINGHAM, MASSACHUSETTS, AND MATRICULATED AT BROWN UNIVERSITY AT AGE 27, AFTER AN ADOLESCENCE OF BLUNT TRAUMA. (HE BECAME MUTE AT THE AGE OF 16, FOLLOWING THE SUICIDE OF HIS MOTHER, AND SPENT THREE YEARS HOSPITALIZED AT MCLEAN HOSPITAL IN BELMONT.) FOLLOWING A STRING OF ODD JOBS, HE BECAME THE VOCALIST FOR THE HARDCORE BAND BLACK HOLE, AND THEN MOVED TO THE U.K., GRADUATING WITH AN M.A. FROM CLARE COLLEGE, CAMBRIDGE. HE HAS WORKED IN THE U.S. AND ABROAD AS A THEATRE DIRECTOR, FURNITURE SALESMAN, DEBT COLLECTOR, PERFORMANCE POET, FARM HAND, HOUSE PAINTER, AND LUMBER TRUCK DRIVER. *VIRGIL'S COW* IS HIS FIRST POETRY COLLECTION. SEVERAL OF ITS POEMS ALSO APPEARED ON THE CD *COMPENDIUM MALEFICARUM III* (INCUNABULUM, 2008), A SPOKEN WORD/ELECTRONIC MUSIC COLLABORATION WITH DAN WARBURTON.

OTHER TITLES FROM MIAMI UNIVERSITY PRESS

POETRY SERIES

GENERAL EDITOR: JAMES REISS

The Bridge of Sighs **STEVE ORLEN**

People Live, They Have Lives **HUGH SEIDMAN**

This Perfect Life **KATE KNAPP JOHNSON**

The Dirt **NANCE VAN WINCKEL**

Moon Go Away, I Don't Love You No More **JIM SIMMERMAN**

Selected Poems: 1965–1995 **HUGH SEIDMAN**

Neither World **RALPH ANGEL**

Now **JUDITH BAUMEL**

Long Distance **ALEDA SHIRLEY**

What Wind Will Do **DEBRA BRUCE**

Kisses **STEVE ORLEN**

Brilliant Windows **LARRY KRAMER**

After a Spell **NANCE VAN WINCKEL**

Kingdom Come **JIM SIMMERMAN**

Dark Summer **MOLLY BENDALL**

The Disappearing Town **JOHN DRURY**

Wind Somewhere, and Shade
KATE KNAPP JOHNSON

The Printer's Error **AARON FOGEL**

Gender Studies **JEFFREY SKINNER**

Ariadne's Island **MOLLY BENDALL**

Burning the Aspern Papers **JOHN DRURY**

Beside Ourselves **NANCE VAN WINCKEL**

GENERAL EDITOR: KEITH TUMA

Rainbow Darkness: an anthology of african american poetry **EDITED BY KEITH TUMA**

Talk Poetry **MAIRÉAD BYRNE**

Between Cup and Lip **PETER MANSON**

Performing Worlds into Being: Native American Women's Theater **EDITED BY A.E. ARMSTRONG, K.L. JOHNSON, AND W.A. WORTMAN**

FICTION SERIES

EDITED BY THE CREATIVE WRITING
FACULTY OF MIAMI UNIVERSITY

Mayor of the Roses **MARIANNE VILLANUEVA**
EDITED BY BRIAN ROLEY

The Waiting Room **ALBERT SGAMBATI**
EDITED BY ERIC GOODMAN

Badlands **CYNTHIA REEVES**
EDITED BY MARGARET LUONGO

A Fight in the Doctor's Office **CARY HOLLADAY**
EDITED BY BRIAN ROLEY